FAIRACRES PUBLIC

JULIAN OF NORWICH
Four Studies

to Commemorate the Sixth Centenary
of the *Revelations of Divine Love*

SLG PRESS
Convent of the Incarnation • Fairacres
Parker Street • Oxford • England
www.slgpress.co.uk

© 2022 SLG PRESS
First Edition 1973
Second Edition 2017
Third Edition 2022

ISBN 978-0-7283-0335-5
ISSN 0307-1405

Line drawings © Sister Rosemary SLG

ACKNOWLEDGEMENTS

We are grateful to Penguin Books Ltd for allowing us to quote liberally from *Revelations of Divine Love,* translated by Clifton Wolters and first published in Penguin Classics in 1966; and for permission to reprint the prayer of St Anselm which is taken from *The Prayers and Meditations of St Anselm,* translated by Sr Benedicta Ward, Penguin Classics, 1973.

The extracts from the poems 'The Last Judgement' and 'The Dream of the Rood' are taken from *Early Christian Poetry,* translated by Charles W. Kennedy, first published by Hollis and Carter and reprinted by Oxford University Press in 1963, to whom our thanks are due for permission to reprint these lines.

The quotations from the Bible, taken from the *Revised Standard Version,* copyrighted 1946 and 1952, are reprinted throughout the article 'Julian of Norwich and the Bible' by kind permission of Thomas Nelson & Sons Ltd.

Finally, we acknowledge with thanks permission to reprint the extract from *Conjectures of a Guilty Bystander* by Thomas Merton, published by Bums and Oates, London 1968, copyright by the Abbey of Gethsemani.

CONTENTS

I saw in my imagination heaven, and our Lord as the head of his own house, who had invited all his dear servants and friends to a great feast. The Lord, I say, occupied no one place in particular in his house, but presided regally over it all, suffusing it with joy and cheer. Utterly at home, and with perfect courtesy, himself was the eternal happiness and comfort of his beloved friends, the marvellous music of his unending love showing in the beauty of his blessed face. Which glorious countenance of the Godhead fills heaven full of joy and delight.

(Ch. 14)

INTRODUCTION

The intention of this book is to serve as an introduction and companion to the reading of the *Revelations of Divine Love* of Julian of Norwich. That work is, on any showing, amongst the most remarkable and beautiful books to be written in our language, and it is certainly one of the first which we know to have been written by a woman. Something of what is says, something of its meaning for today, is explored in these essays, three of which are the work of writers who, though not solitaries, are living a contemplative life in many respects similar to that which Julian herself lived. They bring to their subject an immediate sense of kinship.

Of the extant facts of Julian's life we know very little. She lived as a solitary or anchoress in a little room by the side of St Julian's Church in Norwich. The church, which was seriously damaged during World War II, has been rebuilt, and on the site of the anchorhold there is now a small chapel. We know that Julian was in some way connected with the Benedictine nuns of the nearby abbey of Carrow, and we know for certain one date in her life, 8 May 1373, the day on which she began to have the 'shewings' of God's loving purposes, on which she subsequently reflected for many years, and which form the substance of her book.

There is little more about her of which we can be absolutely sure, and there are many things of which we are uncertain. What does she mean, for instance, when she tells us that she was unlettered? Could she read and write English? It seems probable. Did she know Latin, the language in which most of the theology of her time was written? It seems improbable, though perhaps she had some limited knowledge of it. How was it, as Sister Mary Paul points out, that she seems to have had such an astonishing knowledge of the theology of the New Testament? Did clerical advisers and friends translate the texts for her directly? Was she perhaps in possession of a Wycliffite translation into English?

1

The latter hypothesis is possible, though in view of her devotion to the teaching of the Church, it seems unlikely that she would have possessed a text which she would surely have felt to be tainted with heresy.

There are many other questions to which we should like to know the answers. What for instance were her contacts with the Norwich of her day? We have one brief and tantalising glimpse of Margery Kempe coming to consult her as someone skilled in spiritual matters. We feel sure that there must have been many other such visitors, but we know nothing of them.

Then again it is not only the external facts about her which tend to elude us. There is in the book a kind of mystery which we can neither grasp nor comprehend. She has a way of breaking through our stereotypes and conventions. The life of a solitary, one would imagine, must be cramped and confined. She seems to have a heart and mind which can embrace all humanity, the whole creation. A person who suffers such intense visionary experiences, going so far beyond our everyday consciousness, and reminding us of the hidden depths and heights which exist within each one of us, must surely be intense and strained, if not actually unbalanced. But we find no sense of strain in her. Her book everywhere breathes an extraordinary sanity and good sense.

Again, we might expect that such a peculiarly personal showing of God's love would produce a purely individual statement of Christian beliefs conflicting with the ordinary teaching of the Christian Church at large. But no, Julian shows herself scrupulously careful to respect the common faith of the Church. It is true that she does not fear to meditate on the deepest and most difficult questions concerning God's dealing with humanity, the reality of evil, the hint of the restoration of all things, but she handles these themes with consummate skill and judgement, expressing an insight which is at once personal and corporate, her own and that of the whole tradition.

Theological precision goes hand in hand with warmth and simplicity of human feeling. It seems as though the mystery of human nature, and the mystery of the Christian faith are both of them potentially very different from what we normally imagine them to be in the twenty-first century. Her book gives us greater hope than we normally find easy, and to us, as it did to the greatest poet of our time, it can speak with an unexpected and strengthening authority.

A. M. Allchin

ABBREVIATIONS

The references to *Revelations of Divine Love* throughout the book are to chapters only. In the case of the relatively long chapter fifty-one, however, we have given page numbers to facilitate reference; and these refer to the Penguin Classics edition (see 'Acknowledgements' above).

THE PLACE OF LADY JULIAN OF NORWICH
IN
ENGLISH RELIGIOUS LITERATURE
SISTER EILEEN MARY SLG

And all shall be well
All manner of thing shall be well
When the tongues of flame are in-folded
Into the crowned knot of fire
And the fire and the rose are one.

So ends 'Little Gidding', the last movement of T. S. Eliot's poem *Four Quartets*. In these lines the final image of ultimate unity is prefaced by words which link the poet of the twentieth century with that English anchoress of six centuries before whom we know as the Lady Julian of Norwich. In her own estimation 'a simple and unlettered creature,' she has nevertheless been designated 'the first English woman of letters,'[1] holding a unique place as she does among that company of writers in the vernacular of the fourteenth century which includes Richard Rolle, Walter Hilton, and the author of the *Cloud of Unknowing*, as well as Chaucer and Langland.

'All shall be well and all manner of thing shall be well.' Through the fire and destruction of war-time England, the poet affirms his gospel of optimism and universalism despite the inescapable scandals of evil and suffering. 'Who then devised the torment? Love.'[2] Here too he echoes the Lady Julian, born also into a world of confusion, change and violence, the world of Crécy, the Black Death, the Peasants' Revolt and the rise of

---

[1] Evelyn Underhill in the *Cambridge Medieval History*, Vol. VII (Cambridge University Press, 1932), p. 807.

[2] T. S. Eliot, 'Little Gidding', *Four Quartets* (Faber & Faber, 1943), p. 43.

Lollardry, who could say with equal confidence: 'You would know our Lord's meaning in this thing? Know it well. Love was his meaning' (Ch. 86). Although she does not use Eliot's imagery, yet she would have understood his symbolism of the fire and the rose, the 'reconciliation between the way of Negation and the way of Affirmation, between the practice of austerity and the acceptance of life's revelatory richness, the way of the fire and the way of the rose.'[3] In common with many of her less well-balanced contemporaries, the Lady Julian knows the way of fire, the passion for penance and self-immolation aroused by contact, almost through the physical senses, with Christ's Cross and Passion. 'I wanted his pain to be my pain' (Ch. 3). Yet unlike them she always subordinates pain to love, to compassion, to trust in the eternal providence of God, which is the way of the rose.

In the *Revelations* we have evidence too of a clear, sober intelligence, pondering for thirty years on the divine truths revealed through the successive Shewings of a day and a night. Here there is no sensation-seeking ecstatic, but one whose message is seen increasingly to be relevant today, as T. S. Eliot saw it to be some seventy years ago. Yet for three-and-a-half centuries the Lady Julian was little read by her countrymen, so complete was the break in tone and type of religious writing at the Reformation. It is true that her work was rediscovered and published in the seventeenth century by the English Benedictines who had fled to the Continent and established the Religious Life for English Catholics; yet even in this milieu it was largely forgotten during the next hundred years. It was not until the early years of this century that the few remaining early manuscripts—the earliest dating from the fifteenth century—were brought to light, edited

---

[3] Harry Blamires, *Word Unheard, A Guide through Eliot's* Four Quartets (Barnes & Noble 1969), p. 123.

and republished to become again part of the spiritual heritage of all English Christians.

Yet until the time of the Reformation, that is, for a hundred and fifty years after the original Shewings, the writings of the Lady Julian continued to be popular, especially in certain circles. The novices of Marrick Priory, for example, in H. F. M. Prescott's novel of early sixteenth century England, *The Man on a Donkey*, are seen studying the *Revelations* as part of their spiritual reading.[4] Portrayed here in the setting of a convent just before its dissolution, is a microcosm of that conservative, orthodox world, which nevertheless accepted visions and portents as part of religious experience. Here one can see the relationship between popular religious belief on the eve of the Reformation and its counterpart during the years of abortive reformation in the fourteenth century, with the Lady Julian's relevance in both worlds as a mystical writer, possessing her own personal message which is at the same time always subordinated to the official teaching of the Church.

What place, then, did this anchoress hold among her contemporaries of the English school of mystical writers of the fourteenth century? David Knowles, in common with other historians, accords her a place alongside the author of the *Cloud of Unknowing* (*c*.1360), Richard Rolle (1290–1349) and Walter Hilton (1330–1396). He writes:

> They form a group of which each individual has an independent point of view, though the later among them knew, and owed much to the earlier. They are separated from their predecessors and immediate successors by a number of characteristics; they all wrote in a private capacity and with an intensely individual outlook; they are all in some degree mystical writers, that is to say, they record or prepare for a direct perception of divine

---

[4] H. F. M. Prescott, *The Man on a Donkey* (Eyre & Spottiswoode 1953), pp. 281–2.

action upon the soul outside the limits of ordinary experience; and all wrote at least a part of their works in English.[5]

He goes on to indicate the strong influence of the English eremitical tradition upon these writers, two of whom, Richard Rolle and Julian, were recluses themselves, while Hilton and the unknown author of the *Cloud of Unknowing* wrote their principal treatises for an anchoress and a solitary.

The 'intensely individual outlook' was in part due to the fact that mystical teaching in England at this time was not bound up with any one of the great Religious Orders, as was the case on the Continent, although it could not fail to be influenced by the prevailing religious atmosphere of the day. The Lady Julian would not have been immune from this influence. Trade between Norwich and the Low Countries and Germany flourished, and the teaching of the Rhineland Dominicans, in particular Eckhart and Tauler, would penetrate even to the cell of an anchoress through her spiritual guides or through clients who came to her for help and advice. It is known, for example, that the much-travelled Margery Kempe visited her on at least one occasion in 1413, when Julian was an old and revered woman, knowing that 'she was expert in such things and good counsel could give'.[6]

What were the characteristics of this particular religious climate? It was one in which:

> personal, individual problems and values are supreme, a world in which kinds and degrees of love, divine and human, are matters of earnest debate, together with a search for clarity of conscience and pity for those outside the visible Church, and a

---

[5] David Knowles, *The Religious Orders in England* Vol. II, (Cambridge University Press, 1957), p. 120.

[6] *The Book of Margery Kempe*, quoted by David Knowles in *The English Mystical Tradition* (Burns & Oates, 1961), p. 149.

balancing of the claims of the lives of Martha and Mary, the active and the contemplative.[7]

Most, although not all, of these characteristics appear in the *Revelations*. The whole book is a meditation on a personal vision, brooded upon and developed for thirty years, not in a narcissistic spirit, but in order that it might be shared by the anchoress's even-Christians. 'Throughout all this I was greatly moved with love for my fellow Christians that they might know and see what I was seeing, for I wanted it to cheer them too. The vision was for all and sundry' (Ch. 8).

Again, no one who reads the *Revelations* can fail to notice Julian's Trinitarian preoccupations applied as they are to describe the nature of God, of divine and human love, and the relationship between God and man. When she thinks of the properties of Father, Son and Spirit she speaks of him as Maker, Keeper and Lover; she knows him as Almighty, All-Wise, All-Good (Ch. 5), and as Light, Love and Life (Ch. 83). He functions too in a Trinitarian fashion: 'The Father may, the Son can, the Holy Ghost will do whatever it is he wills' (Ch. 31). Created beings share these attributes of the Trinity when they are being true to themselves: 'Thus was my understanding led on by God to realize and to know that our soul is a trinity—only created—like the blessed uncreated Trinity' (Ch. 55). We possess reason, insight and love (Ch. 56), and experience God through nature, mercy and grace (Ch. 58). Through grace comes 'the wound of true contrition, the wound of genuine compassion and the wound of sincere longing for God' (Ch. 2). All this leads to a three-fold charity. 'I understood this light of Charity in three ways: charity as uncreated; charity as created; and charity as given. Untreated charity is God; created charity is our soul in God; given charity is virtue' (Ch. 84).

---

[7] David Knowles, *The English Mystical Tradition*, op. cit., p. 43.

Yet again, in the long thirteenth revelation, which occupies chapters 27–30 of her book, Julian is seen struggling with the tensions and contradictions arising from the existence of sin in a world ruled by a God of Love:

> Another part of our same belief is that many creatures will be damned; for example, the angels who fell from heaven through pride, and are now fiends; and those men on earth who die apart from the Faith of Holy Church, namely, the heathen; and those too, who are christened but live unchristian lives, and so die out of love—all these shall be condemned to hell everlastingly, as Holy Church teaches me to believe. This being so I thought it quite impossible that everything should turn out well, as our Lord was now showing me. (Ch. 32)

In the end she receives her assurance within the context of the Church's teaching. Yet in the struggle between individual conscience and orthodox belief she shows herself to be a true child of her age, and of ours. If there is not a similar tension between the claims of Martha and Mary it is because she has found a unity in her own vocation which transcends both.

Despite her affinity with other English writers of her generation, Julian retains her own individual characteristics and style. In contrast to women visionaries on the Continent such as Mechtild of Magdeburg, Bridget of Sweden and Catherine of Siena, who occupied positions of influence in the world of their day, Julian was born into an England which looked with disfavour on the spiritual revelations of women. She protests against this convention: 'Because I am a woman should I therefore believe that I ought not to tell you about the goodness of God, since I saw at the same time that it is his will that it be known?' (Ch. 6, Shorter Version) The fact that this prejudice exists may be one reason why she does not set out to be a teacher indicating a methodical scheme by which men might draw near to God, nor does she give ultimate visions of the Absolute as many of her contemporaries did. She simply records a Revelation, prepared for by faith and held in faith. It is noticeable that there is no mention of preliminary ascetical exercises in her writing, only an insistence on the necessity of 'cleaving' or 'clinging' to the goodness of God. All commentators speak of the influence of the *Ancrene Riwle* on the Lady Julian, yet this text-book for recluses, written in the early years of the thirteenth century, is largely concerned with such inner and outer ascetical preparations for prayer. These, one supposes, are taken for granted in Julian's case, since there is no doubt that such practices must have played a part in her life.

If one is to look at the influence of the *Ancrene Riwle* on Julian it can perhaps be found in the devotions prescribed for anchoresses which occupy the first chapter of the book and in the allegory of the Lord and His Beloved which can be placed alongside Julian's own image of the Lord and His Servant. It has been said of the Lady Julian that 'she is in many ways more like a painter than a writer; she sees pictures and communicates them by means of language.'[8] In the *Ancrene Riwle,* the five morning greetings before the crucifix in memory of Christ's wounds, and the noon prayer in memory of the Passion, which were to be said daily, must have impressed the original vision repeatedly upon her mind in pictorial form:

> Ah, Jesus, grant me thy mercy; Jesus hung on the Cross for my sins, by those five wounds from which thou didst bleed, heal my soul, bleeding from all the sins with which it has been wounded through my five senses. Grant this in remembrance of thy wounds dear Lord.[9]

Similarly, one recognises Julian's arithmetical methods of statement in the prayer to the Trinity prescribed for the anchoress's noon-day devotions:

---

[8] Elizabeth Jennings, *Every Changing Shape*, (Deutsch 1961), p. 46.
[9] *The Ancrene Riwle,* trans. M. B. Salu (Burns & Oates 1955), p. 11.

Grant me, O One Almighty God, threefold in three Persons, these same three things power to serve Thee, wisdom to please Thee, love and will to bring these into action, strength that I may act, wisdom that I may know how to act, love that I may desire to perform always what is most pleasing to Thee.[10]

In Julian's image of the Lord and His Servant (Chs 51–52) the willing servant is Christ, representative of Everyman, while the Lord is God the Father. In the *Ancrene Riwle* the lady is the stubborn human soul being wooed by Christ the Lord.

The resemblance between the two allegories lies in the language of chivalry in which they are written, in the courtesy of the Lord, his respect for the freedom of the Beloved, his compassion and patience. Yet Julian's is the denser image, containing as it does the whole doctrine of the recapitulation of the human race in Christ, which might have been taken directly from the teaching of Irenaeus.

Commentators have written at length on other influences from the immediate and remote past to be discerned in Julian's work. They include the schemes of thought developed by Plotinus, Augustine, Dionysius the Areopagite, the Victorines, Ruysbroeck and other writers of the twelfth and thirteenth centuries, notably St Anselm, whose teaching on the motherhood of Christ Julian made her own. Yet apart from these distinguished names there is in the genealogy of English religious literature a line which connects Julian with the first flowering of English vernacular writing in Anglo-Saxon between the seventh century and the Norman Conquest. As far as religious prose and poetry was concerned, this line was never broken, for homilies of Bede, Aelfric and Wulfstan were being transcribed long after the middle of the eleventh century, while pre-Conquest English poems remain which contain the seeds of that warm medieval devotion to

---

[10] *The Ancrene Riwle,* p. 10.

Christ's humanity which is the mark of Julian and her contemporaries. Often it has to be sought for in terrifying epic passages of doom and judgement, as for example in an eighth century poem on the Last Judgement in which the Christ whom the Lady Julian would have known emerges out of a context of vengeance and violence:

> Then comes the wondrous presence of Christ,
> The glory of the Great King, from the eastern skies.
> … To all the good He is gracious of aspect,
> Winsome and blithe to that holy band,
> Joyous and loving, a gentle Friend.
> 'Tis a pleasant sight and sweet to His dear ones,
> That shining beauty gentle in joy,
> The coming of the Saviour, the King of might.[11]

Again one can compare Julian's vision of the Cross with the following lines from the same poem:

> The Rood of our Saviour red with His blood, Over-run with bright gore, upreared before men,
> With radiant light shall illumine the wide Creation. No shadows shall lurk where the light of the Cross Streams on all nations.

In particular one sees the ancestry of Julian's visions in that eighth century poem of passionate adoration of the Cross, the Dream of the Rood:

> Many a bale I bore on that hill-side
> Seeing the Lord in agony outstretched.
> Black darkness covered with clouds God's body,
> That radiant splendour. Shadow went forth
> Wan under heaven; all creation wept
> Bewailing the King's death. Christ was on the Cross.[12]

---

[11] 'The Last Judgement' from *Early English Christian Poetry*, edited by Charles W. Kennedy (Oxford University Press, 1963), p. 269.
[12] 'The Dream of the Rood' from *Early English Christian Poetry*, p. 94.

Alongside of this one can read Lady Julian, absorbed in the same theme: 'All creatures capable of suffering pain suffered with him; I mean, all creatures that God has made for our use. Even heaven and earth languished for grief in their own peculiar way when Christ died' (Ch. 18).

Her style also blends rhetorical and other devices of her own day with the alliterative phrases of Early English poetry in a way which is not forced or artificial but obviously part of her own normal daily speech. To this Julian has added her own contribution in vivid imagery and convincing circumstantial detail to reveal almost incidentally to posterity her lively mind and lovable personality.

So on the six-hundredth anniversary of her Shewings we see the Lady Julian standing at a watershed of English religious literature, pointing forward to the present day when her message of confidence and love is needed as never before, and looking back for an equal length of time to those who first found in the English tongue a vehicle for the expression of their religious longings and fears.

Across the centuries she would give to us all the message with which her *Revelations* close:

> And I saw for certain, both here and elsewhere, that before ever he made us, God loved us; and that his love has never slackened, nor ever shall. In this love all his works have been done, and in this love he has made everything serve us; and in this love our life is everlasting. Our beginning was when we were made, but the love in which he made us never had beginning. In it we have our beginning.
>
> All this we shall see in God for ever. May Jesus grant this. Amen.   (Ch. 86)

*Ponder carefully the range of this word
EVER. It describes the height of the love Christ
knew for our salvation, and the manifold joys that
flow from the passion. For example, he rejoices that
the deed is past and done, and he shall suffer no
more; he rejoices too that he has raised us to heaven,
and made us to be his crown and eternal delight;
again, he rejoices that by his passion he has bought
us out from the eternal pain of hell.* (Ch. 23)

JULIAN OF NORWICH AND THE BIBLE
SISTER MARY PAUL SLG

The definitely-known facts about Julian of Norwich's life can be told in one brief paragraph. The definitely-known fact about Julian and the Bible can be put in one short sentence: *Revelations of Divine Love* is a book written by a person steeped in biblical thought, particularly that of the New Testament, and especially that of the Pauline and Johannine writings.

> For God so loved the world that he gave his only Son that whoever believes in him should not perish but have eternal life. For God sent the Son into the world, not to condemn the world, but that the world might be saved through him.   (John 3:16–17)

> Now is the judgement of this world, now shall the ruler of this world be cast out; and I, when I am lifted up from the earth, will draw all men to myself.   (John 12:31–31)

> So we know and believe the love God has for us. God is love, and he who abides in love abides in God, and God abides in him. In this is love perfected with us, that we may have confidence for the day of judgement, because as he is so are we in this world.
> (1 John 4:16–17)

These words serve well to summarize Julian's teaching on the love of God and his purpose to draw all men to himself. Her vision of Christ is of cosmic dimensions. Without ever losing sight of Christ's love for each person—a love which she experienced profoundly—she stresses the corporate nature of Christ's reconciliation and re-creation of mankind. Like St Paul she sees the oneness of man in Adam, and the oneness of restored mankind in Christ, himself true man, true Adam. Her thought and prayer breathe the atmosphere of the New Testament. Christ on the cross thirsts for all mankind. This thirst of Christ for 'all souls to be saved', 'all of mankind who are to be saved', or 'man-who-is-to-be-saved', as she variously expresses it, is one of the primary

16

themes of her book. Many times she says that the revelations of God's love which she received were not for herself alone but for all her 'fellow-Christians'. God's purpose, Christ's thirst, is for the bliss of all humanity. Whether in fact every human being will ultimately respond to God's love is an open question, a troubling one with which she grapples, but which she has to leave unresolved. God *desires* the salvation of all mankind whom he has created in love.

It needs to be stressed that in the background of everything Julian says is the passion of Christ. Her visions form the basis of every theological statement she makes. Throughout the time that she with her 'inward sight' was especially considering the goodness of God in creation, for example, she 'seemed to see with [her] actual eyes' the head of Jesus as it appeared at the time of the crucifixion (Ch. 7). It is in the light of the passion of the God-Man that she understands all the truths of the Christian revelation and of the particular revelations which she received. St Paul once determined 'to know nothing except Jesus Christ and him crucified' (1 Cor. 2:2), and from that perspective he expounded the whole mystery of Christ in the creation, redemption, and transfiguration of all things. Julian also, eyes fixed on the crucified, sees (in Paul's words): 'the breadth and length and height and depth', and knows 'the love of Christ which surpasses knowledge'. For her, as for him, it is through God's Spirit, and because Christ 'dwells in [her] heart through faith' and she is 'rooted and grounded in love' that she comprehends the Christian revelation in its totality, in its cosmic dimensions and its universal significance (see Eph. 3:14–19).

There are several major paradoxes in Julian's writing, as there are in the New Testament. The first paradox is that between creation's magnificence, the wonder of all God has made, and the great reverence and love the Christian therefore has toward it; and creation's smallness, its insignificance in comparison with the Creator. Julian's renunciation of the world, her withdrawal from the ordinary life of her day into the cell of an anchoress, was positive; it was the result of knowing God, not the result of hating creation. Hatred of creation would, indeed, be blasphemous in view of God's love for it. Julian returns to the theme of creation many times, but she sets the theme in Chapter five:

> It was at this time that our Lord showed me spiritually how intimately he loves us. I saw that he is everything that we know to be good and helpful. In his love he clothes us, enfolds and embraces us; that tender love completely surrounds us, never to leave us. As I saw it he is everything that is good.
>
> And he showed me more, a little thing, the size of a hazelnut, on the palm of my hand, round like a ball. I looked at it thoughtfully and wondered, 'What is this?' And the answer came, 'It is all that is made'. I marvelled that it continued to exist and did not suddenly disintegrate; it was so small. And again my mind supplied the answer, 'It exists, both now and for ever, because God loves it.' In short, everything owes its existence to the love of God.
>
> In this 'little thing' I saw three truths. The first is that God made it; the second is that God loves it; and the third is that God sustains it.

The first paradox inherent in creation is that between its greatness (made, sustained and loved by God) and its smallness. The second paradox, made more explicit in other passages, is that between the goodness of God manifested in creation and the reality of evil which is also manifested within the created order. This paradox is expressed in the New Testament, and perhaps nowhere more strikingly than in the Johannine writings. The fourth Gospel opens with a poem on the creation of the world through the *Logos* of God who was with God 'in the beginning', who indeed *was* God. 'In him was life, and the life was the light of men' (1:4). It is this *Logos*, the Son, the only begotten, whom God gave to the world because 'God so loved the world' (3:16).

In seeming contradiction to God's love for the world, Christians are admonished: 'Do not love the world or the things in the world. If anyone loves the world, love for the Father is not in him' (2:15). But the writer immediately shows what he means by adding: 'For all that is in the world, the lust of the flesh and the lust of the eyes and the pride of life, is not of the Father but is of the world. And the world passes away, and the lust of it' (2:16–17). He is speaking of the world, the creation, in its estrangement from God its Creator, for 'the whole world is in the power of the evil one' (5:19). This, in Pauline language, is 'the prince of the power of the air, the spirit that is now at work in the sons of disobedience' (Eph. 2:2). The world, in the state in which we know it, is ambiguous. As Julian says in summing up her first revelation, she saw 'the whole creation—I was well aware that the universe is great and huge, beautiful and good' (Ch. 8). But it is a world in which there is a mystery of evil at work, a power of evil that could only be overcome by the work of the same Logos who acted in creation. Julian speaks of 'his holy incarnation, his precious blood, his holy passion, his most dear death and wounds' (Ch. 6), in connection with the first revelation. As the writer of I John says, 'God is light and in him is no darkness at all' (1:5); this corresponds to Julian's insistence that 'God is all that is good and himself is the goodness of all good things' (Ch. 8). The next words of 1 John, 'the blood of Jesus his Son cleanses us from all sin' (1:7), correspond to Julian's:

> And at once I saw the red blood trickling down from under the garland, hot, fresh, and plentiful, just as it did at the time of his passion when the crown of thorns was pressed on to the blessed head of God-and-Man, who suffered for me.   (Ch. 4)

This phrase 'suffered for me' sounds like a pietistic individualistic statement; and so, no doubt, it is; for Julian never lost sight of her personal relationship to her Saviour. Nevertheless, she stresses the universal and corporate aspect of Christ's redemption:

The most precious blood of our Lord Jesus Christ is in truth both costly and copious. Look and see. The costly and copious flood of his most precious blood streamed down into hell, and burst the chains, and freed all there who belonged to the Court of Heaven. The costly and copious flood of his most precious blood overflows the whole of earth, and is available to wash all creatures (if they are willing) from their sin, present, past, or future. The costly and copious flood of his most precious blood ascends up to heaven, to our Lord's blessed body itself, and is found there in him, who bleeds and pleads for us with the Father—and that for as long as need shall require, For ever it flows through all heaven, rejoicing to save mankind, such as are there already and those who are yet to come, making up the number of the saints. (Ch. 12)

'For,' says Julian in another chapter, 'the fundamental thing about the passion is to consider who he is who has suffered. I began to think about the majesty and the greatness of his glorious Godhead, now united with his precious, tender body' (Ch. 20). As, in Johannine language, it was he 'through whom all things were made' who suffered, Julian says that all things suffered when he suffered. 'Even heaven and earth languished for grief in their own peculiar way when Christ died' (Ch. 18). 'We know that the whole creation has been groaning in travail together until now' (Rom. 8:22). Julian, too, sees the moment of the passion as the supreme moment of passion for the creation.

We know from our creed, and believe through the teaching and preaching of Holy Church, that the blessed Trinity makes mankind in his image and likeness. In the same way we know that when man fell so deeply and wretchedly through sin there was no other help forthcoming to restore him but from him who made man. And he who out of love made man, by the same love would restore him not merely to his former bliss but to one that was even greater. Just as we were made like the Trinity at our first creation, so our Maker would have us like our Saviour Jesus Christ, in heaven for ever by virtue of our re-creation.

> Between these two creations he willed — out of love for man —
> to make himself as like man, in all our wretchedness and filth, as
> is possible without sin. (Ch. 10)

This last sentence brings to mind Philippians 2, as does also the remarkable allegory of the Lord and his servant in Chapter 51 of Julian's book. In the re-creation Julian stresses is the unity of all in Christ:

> It is upon this unity that all those of mankind who are to be saved
> must depend. God, as I see it, is everything that is good; he has
> made the whole of creation, and loves all that he has made. And
> whoever loves his fellow Christians for God, loves all there is.
> For everything is included in the 'mankind who are to be saved:'
> everything, I say, that has been created, and the maker of all as
> well! For God is in man, and God is in everything. (Ch. 9)

The following lines from Chapter 55 reflect the thought of Ephesians (4:11–13) and are a good example of how Julian has absorbed the biblical teaching and made it her own, for here as usual she does not quote directly:

> The gifts that God makes to his creatures he has given to his Son
> Jesus on our behalf. And he who indwells us retains these gifts
> until we are full grown in body and soul alike, each contributing
> its due share until by natural process we are spiritually mature.
> Then the natural foundation, with mercy's cooperation, will be
> inbreathed by the grace of the Holy Spirit with gifts that lead to
> eternal life.

The Problem of Evil

'I saw the whole Godhead concentrated as it were in a single point, and thereby I learnt that he is in all things' (Ch. 11). As Julian considered God 'in all things' she was thinking, 'What is sin?' She did not receive a direct answer; rather she saw that 'all is through the foresight and wisdom of God' and,

Everything that is done is well done, for it is our Lord God who does it. God is the focal point of everything, and he does it all. And I was sure he does no sin! From this I gathered that sin is not a thing that we do, not a deed, for in all that was *done,* there was no sin showed. (Ch. 11)

She continues in a way as uncompromising as St Paul in Romans to expound the doctrine of God's providence:

All … is in accordance with the nature and plan that God has decided for everything from before creation … I saw with absolute certainty that he never changes his purpose in anything whatever, and never will. Through his ordering everything has been known to him from the first. (Ch. 11)

Julian insists that: 'There is no doer but he', and St Paul explicitly states that 'God has consigned all men to disobedience, that he may have mercy on all' (Rom. 11:32). Like Julian, who says: 'He showed me all this to my great happiness' (Ch. 11), St Paul immediately breaks into a hymn of praise: 'O the depth of the riches and wisdom and knowledge of God! How unsearchable are his judgements and how inscrutable his ways!' (Rom. 11:33).

Julian's doctrine of God's almightiness and absolute sovereignty of his creation is completely biblical. If God were not fully in control of the created order then, looking out on the world, we would have cause to despair. Julian holds firmly to this doctrine and, looking out on the world's only too obvious sin and evil, asks what, then, *is* sin and evil?

In my foolish way I had often wondered why the foreseeing wisdom of God could not have prevented the beginning of sin, for then, thought I, all would have been well. … Jesus answered, 'Sin was necessary; but all shall be well, and all shall be well, and all manner of thing shall be well.'

Chapter 27 is one of the passages in the Shewings where the correspondence with the thought of St Paul is so close that it seemed useful to intersperse his words with hers.

In this simple word *sin* our Lord reminded me in a general sort of way of all that is not good: the despicable shame and utter self-denial he endured for us, both in his life and in his dying.

... who, though he was in the form of God, did not count equality with God a thing to be grasped, but emptied himself, taking the form of a servant, being born in the likeness of men. And being found in human form he humbled himself and became obedient unto death, even death on a cross. (Phil. 2:6–8)

And of all the suffering and pain of his creation, both spiritual and physical.

For the creation waits with eager longing for the revealing of the sons of God; for the creation was subjected to futility, not of its own will but by the will of him who subjected it in hope; because the creation itself will be set free from its bondage to decay and obtain the glorious liberty of the children of God. We know that the whole creation has been groaning in travail together until now. (Rom. 8:19–22)

For all of us have already experienced something of this abnegation and we have to deny ourselves as we follow our master Jesus, until we are wholly cleansed. I mean, until this body of death and our inward affections (which are not very good) are completely done away.

Not only the creation, but we ourselves, who have the first fruits of the Spirit, groan inwardly as we wait for adoption as sons, the redemption of our bodies. (Rom. 8:23)

All this I saw, together with all the suffering that ever has been or can be. And of all pain I understood that the passion of Christ was the greatest and most surpassing. All this was shown in a flash, and quickly passed over into consolation—for our good Lord would not have the soul frightened by this ugly sight.

Evil, sin, suffering and pain are vividly real to Julian. This is one aspect of truth which must be borne in mind when she goes on to say, 'But I did not see *sin*. I believe it has no substance or real existence. It can only be known by the pain it causes'

(Ch. 27). Neither the Bible nor Julian gives a philosophical rationale of evil. They give the facts of revelation, and Christian philosophers have pondered on these facts. Julian is content to say, in respect of sin having 'no manner of substance nor no part of being,'

> In these words I saw one of God's marvellously deep secrets—a secret which he will plainly reveal to us in heaven. And when we know it we will see the reason why he allowed sin to come, and seeing, we shall rejoice in him for ever.

St Paul often uses the word *musterion*, translated 'mystery' in the Revised Standard Version and 'secret' in some translations. It means a secret of a special kind, a secret hidden in the depths of God's own counsel which only he can reveal and which, even when it is revealed, remains a great mystery, something with depths of meaning far beyond what the human mind can fathom. Paul says that he is a minister whose function is 'to make the word of God fully known, the mystery hidden for ages and generations but now made manifest to his saints. To them God chose to make known how great among the Gentiles are the riches of the glory of this mystery, which is Christ in you, the hope of glory' (Col. 1:25–27; cf. Eph. 3:1–13). It is this hope, this eschatological hope, which informs all of Julian's faith. The manifestation of Christ, the fact of his indwelling presence, is God's secret, God's own mystery which is in process of being revealed to the Christian believer. The revelation will not be complete until 'the day of Jesus Christ' (Phil.1:6) in the age 'which is to come' (Eph. 1:21). Julian is in the heart of this Pauline theology when she says:

> For I saw (as I already knew by our faith) that there will be an end to pain and sorrow for those to be saved. And we shall receive not only the same bliss that souls in heaven already know, but a new one in addition, which will flow in abundance from God and fill us to the brim. These are the good things that he has

planned to give us from the very first. They are now stored and hidden within himself, for till that time comes no creature is fit enough or capable of receiving them. (Ch. 75)

Our 'Godly Will'

There is a further paradox related to the primary paradox between God's 'all shall be well' and the existence of evil which is the paradox between a person's sinfulness and their 'godly will'. The former paradox concerns the universal problem of evil, the latter one the particular problem of evil in each person. This is a complex matter and it is impossible to do full justice to Julian in a few brief quotations. Her convictions are built up during a long dialogue with God in the course of which she fearlessly expresses all that troubles her mind, particularly a seeming inconsistency between the teaching of the Church and the teaching she received in the revelations. She refuses to reject either, holding them in a tension which is resolved at a deeper level of trust in God himself.

> In every soul to be saved is a godly will that has never consented to sin, in the past or in the future. Just as there is an animal will in our lower nature that does not will what is good, so there is a godly will in our higher part, which by its basic goodness never wills what is evil, but only what is good. (Ch. 37)

Julian does not say that we are to be saved or that no one has ever consented to sin in the 'higher part'. The question whether there are souls in hell is one which she has to leave open. There *may* be such. What she does say is that in *'every soul to be saved* is a godly will'. The saved, those who are already living in Christ and Christ in them, experience tension between their 'godly will' that wills, or at least desires to will, the will of God and the psychic forces of memory and imagination, of unreasonable emotion, of perverse reactions that lead to failures and sins, small and great. St Paul expressed this dilemma and its resolution when he said:

I do not understand my own actions. For I do not do what I want, but I do the very thing I hate. ... For I know that nothing good dwells within me, that is, in my flesh. I can will what is right, but I cannot do it. For I do not do the good I want, but the evil I do not want is what I do. Now if I do what I do not want, it is no longer I that do it, but sin which dwells within me. ... Wretched man that I am! Who will deliver me from this body of death? Thanks be to God through Jesus Christ our Lord!

(Rom. 7:15; 18–19; 24–25)

It is Christ himself who keeps the Christian 'securely', even though he sins. In Chapter 39, Julian says:

Our courteous Lord does not want his servants to despair even if they fall frequently and grievously. Our falling does not stop his loving us. Peace and love are always at work in us, but we are not always in peace and love. But he wants us in this way to realize that he is the foundation of the whole of our life in love, and furthermore that he is our eternal protector, and mighty defender against our enemies who are so very fierce and wicked.

For we are not contending against flesh and blood, but against the principalities, against the powers, against the world rulers of this present darkness, against the spiritual hosts of wickedness in the heavenly places. (Eph. 6:12)

And, alas, our need is all the greater since we give them every opportunity by our failures. (Ch. 39)

Nevertheless:

If we never fell, we should never know how weak and wretched we are in ourselves; nor should we ever appreciate the astonishing love of our Maker ... It is a good thing to know this. Another benefit is the sense of insignificance and humbling that we get by seeing ourselves fall. Through it, as we know, we shall be raised up to heaven: but such exaltation might never have been ours without the prior humbling. (Ch. 61)

Christ has been *highly* exalted because of his self-humbling (Phil. 2:8–9); the Christian is humbled through realization that God continues to love him in spite of his sins. This realization must not be made an excuse for sinning. Julian is explicit on this point, as is St Paul, in spite of which they are both liable to mis-understanding. Julian says:

> But if, because of all this spiritual comfort we have been talking of, one were foolish enough to say, "If this is true, it is a good thing to sin because the reward will be greater", or to hold sin to be less sinful, then beware! Should such a thought come it would be untrue, and would stem from the enemy of the very love that tells of all this comfort. (Ch. 40)

And St Paul says:

> What shall we say then? Are we to continue in sin that grace may abound? By no means! ... Do you not know that all of us who have been baptized into Christ Jesus were baptized into his death? We were buried therefore with him by baptism into death, so that as Christ was raised from the dead by the glory of the Father, we too might walk in newness of life.
>
> So you also must consider yourselves dead to sin and alive to God in Christ Jesus. Let not sin therefore reign in your mortal bodies ... but yield yourselves to God as men who have been brought from death to life. ... Thanks be to God, that you who were once slaves of sin have become obedient from the heart to the standard of teaching to which you were committed.
> (Rom. 6, *passim*)

In line with this thought of obedience from the heart, Julian says:

> The same blessed love teaches us that we should hate sin for Love's sake alone. I am quite clear about this: the more a soul sees this in the courtesy and love of our Lord God, the more he hates to sin, and the greater is his sense of shame. (Ch. 40)

The Lord and the Servant

It is in chapter fifty-one in 'the mysterious and wonderful illustration of the lord who had a servant' that Julian expresses the essence of her theological understanding of our destiny in Christ. This understanding came to her during twenty years of prayerfully pondering the initial revelation. So much biblical richness appears in this one fairly long chapter that I will limit my attention to two important and interrelated biblical themes: the 'servant' and the 'second Adam'.

In some of the poems that appear in Isaiah 40–55, poems written during the exile of the Jews in Babylon, the mysterious figure of a servant appears, a servant who, in the fifty-third chapter, is portrayed as one who 'poured out his soul to death, and was numbered with the transgressors; yet he bore the sin of many, and made intercession for the transgressors' (Isa. 53:12). Sometimes the servant is an individual and sometimes Israel as a whole. The servant is Israel in its role as the elect of God called to be 'a light to the nations, that my salvation may reach to the end of the earth' (49:6). The servant is also the faithful individual, often the lonely prophet, in whom and through whom God's purpose is furthered when the people as a whole is unfaithful. The faithful prophet is never a *mere* individual: insofar as he is faithful to God's call to Israel, he *is* Israel. But no prophet could fully respond to God's call to be 'a light to the nations' or to be the means by which God's salvation would 'reach to the end of the earth', for even the greatest prophets were members of sinful humanity (members of Adam in the biblical sense). Ultimately only God himself could save both Israel and the 'nations'. 'Turn to me and be saved, all the ends of the earth! For I am God, and there is no other' (Isa. 45:22). The New Testament writers see Christ, God incarnate, the new Adam, as the servant in whom God fulfils his purpose for mankind. Christ is the new man, the new humanity, into whom all men are called to be incorporated, and those who have borne the image of the earthly Adam now, after their baptism into Christ, bear the image of the heavenly Adam, that is, the image and likeness of God in which humanity was originally created.[13]

All this and much more is the background of Julian's understanding of the servant whom she saw 'first in my spirit in physical outline' and later 'more spiritually without any such outline' (Ch. 51).

The servant 'who stood before his Lord I understood to be Adam, There was shown at that time just one man and his fall; to make us understand that God sees Everyman and his fall. In the sight of God everyman is one man, and one man is everyman.' (Ch. 51). 'Adam for Paul is "mankind", "everyman", Paul himself.'[114] The servant seen by Julian is not only Adam, fallen humanity, but Christ:

> In the *servant* is represented the second Person of the Trinity; and in the servant again Adam or, in other words, Everyman. When I speak of the *Son* I am thinking of the Godhead which is equal to the Father's, and when I say the servant I have Christ's human nature in mind. He is the true Adam.
>
> When Adam *fell*, God's Son fell. Because of the true unity which had been decreed in heaven, God's Son could not be dissociated from Adam. By *Adam* I always understand, Everyman. Adam fell from life to death, first into the depths of this wretched world, and then into hell. God's Son fell, with Adam, but into the depth of the Virgin's womb—herself the fairest daughter of Adam—with the intent of excusing Adam from blame both in heaven and on earth. And with a mighty arm he brought him out of hell. By the servant's *wisdom* and *goodness* the Son is understood. The *poor clothes* of the workman ... is a reference to human nature, and Adam, and all the subsequent mischief and

---

[13] Alan Richardson, *An Introduction to the Theology of the New Testament*, (SCM Press, 1958), p. 248.

[14] Ibid.

weakness. In all this the good Lord showed his own Son and Adam as one man. Our virtue and goodness are due to Jesus Christ, our weakness and blindness to Adam; and both were shown in the one servant. In this way we can *see* how our good Lord Jesus has taken upon himself all our blame, and that, as a result, our Father cannot and will not blame us more than his own dear Son, Jesus Christ.   (Ch. 51)

Christ, the God-Man, is here seen as the servant who, in the poem of Isaiah is said to have borne 'the sin of many and made intercession for the transgressors' (53:12c). 'By his knowledge shall the righteous one, my servant, make many to be accounted righteous; and he shall bear their iniquities.' (53:11b). And the author of Hebrews says:

> Consequently, when Christ came into the world, he said, Sacrifices and burnt offerings thou hast not desired, but a body hast thou prepared for me; in burnt offerings and sin offerings thou hast taken no pleasure. Then I said, 'Lo, I have come to do thy will, O God', as it is written of me in the roll of the book.
> (Heb. 10:5–7)

As if these words were in her mind, Julian continues:

> So the servant, before he came to this world *stood before* his Father, ready for his will and against the time he should be *sent* to do that most worthy deed by which mankind was brought back to heaven. And this, notwithstanding he is God, equal with his Father in respect of his Godhead. In his future purpose he was to be Man, to save man by fulfilling his Father's will.   (Ch. 51)

For, as St Paul says,

> He [God the Father] chose us in him [Christ] before the foundation of the world. ... He destined us in love to be his sons through Jesus Christ, according to the purpose of his will, to the praise of his glorious grace which he freely bestowed on us in the Beloved. In him we have redemption through his blood, the

forgiveness of our trespasses, according to the riches of his grace
which he lavished upon us.   (Eph. 1:4–8.)

The whole of chapter fifty-one of *Revelations of Divine Love*
contains concise and precise theology, echoing many biblical
passages. The pictorial descriptions are the background to intel-
lectualized truths. Julian concludes the chapter by saying:

> Now sits the Son, the labourer no longer standing on the Father's
> left, but sitting at the Father's right, in eternal peace and rest. (We
> do not mean, of course, that the Son sits literally on the right
> hand, side by side as people sit here! As I see it there is nothing
> of this sort in the Holy Trinity. 'To sit at the Father's right hand'
> means that he enjoys the highest dignity with the Father.) Now
> is the Bridegroom, God's Son, resting with his beloved wife, the
> beautiful Virgin, eternally joyful. Now sits the Son, true God and
> true man, at rest and in peace in his own *city*, that city prepared
> for him in the eternal purpose of the Father. And the Father in
> the Son and the Holy Spirit in the Father and in the Son.
>   (Ch. 51)

It was in this illustration of a lord and his servant that Julian
came to understand how it is that God is not wroth with us,
though we are so manifestly sinful and blameworthy:

> I saw that God never *began* to love mankind: for just as mankind
> is going to enjoy unending bliss and thereby delight God with
> regard to his handiwork, so, in the providence and intention of
> God, has mankind been known and loved from everlasting. For
> with the eternal consent and approval of the whole Trinity, the
> second Person willed to become the foundation and the head of
> this lovely human nature. From him we come, with him we are
> included, to him we go, in him we shall find all heaven and last-
> ing joy — all by the foreseeing purpose of the whole Trinity from
> before time. … And what we are going to be forever, as such we
> have been treasured and hidden by God, known and loved from
> before time. Therefore he wants us to realize that the noblest
> thing he has ever made is mankind, and its complete expression

and perfect example is the blessed soul of Christ. Moreover he would have us understand that his precious human soul was inseparably united to him when his humanity was made, and the union is so skilful and strong that this human soul is united to God, and thereby made holy forever. More, he wills us to know that all souls to be saved in heaven for ever are joined and united in this union, and made holy in this holiness.   (Ch. 53)

It is this union *with Christ*, this holiness *of Christ*, that assures us that there is that in us which does not assent to sin, though we are buffeted by temptation and fall into actual sin by our weakness (the weakness we continue to know as members of Adam). Julian is very realistic in her description of the spiritual life (see Chapter 82, for example). To use St Paul's words, 'For as in Adam all die, so also in Christ shall all be made alive' (1 Cor.15:22). For Julian, as for Paul, it is the literal incorporation of human beings into Jesus, who is fully human as well as fully divine, that guarantees our ultimate destiny: our fulfilment, our sanctification and, rightly understood, our 'deification' as the Fathers of the Church spoke of it. As Julian says: 'Individuals may often break down—or so it seems to them—but the whole body of Holy Church is unbreakable, whether in the past, present, or future. So it is a good, sound, grace-bringing thing to resolve, humbly but firmly, to be fastened and united to Holy Church our Mother—in other words, to Jesus Christ' (Ch. 61)

Conclusion

In Julian's visions of Christ's passion, the visions from which all her insight flowed, we see the source of her understanding of the universality of God's purpose accomplished in Christ:

With a glad countenance our Lord looked at his side, rejoicing as he gazed. And as he looked, I, with my limited understanding, was led by way of this same wound into his side. There he showed me a place, fair and delightful, large enough for all saved mankind to rest in peace and love. (Ch. 24)

For his goodness enfolds every one of his creatures and all his blessed works, eternally and surpassingly. For he himself is eternity, and has made us for himself alone, has restored us by his blessed passion, and keeps us in his blessed love. And all because he is goodness. (Ch. 5)

MOTHER JULIAN
Barbara Bishop

A little thing you showed her, the size of a hazelnut;
　　On the palm of her hand, round like a ball it lay.
'What is it,' she said, 'this little fragile thing?'
　　　'It is all that is made,' you said, 'and exists now and forever
　　　for I love it.'
This little fragile thing, all that is made—
　　Thousands of millions of galaxies, billions of billions of stars
　　whirling in immeasurable space, limitless-seeming, incomprehensible;
　　vast, unimaginably vast: brain-whirling, mind-numbing
　　(yet sparkling in simple beauty on mountain lake)
　　　　because you love it all.
These little things—
　　Microscopic Diatomaceae, primal sea plants:
　　fifteen thousand intricate designs, infinitesimally small
　　designs, maintained through millions of years:
　　　　such beauty for earth's basic food!
　　　　such lavish waste, such prodigality!
　　　　　because you love earth so.
These fragile things—
　　Strange animal creatures, two-footed furless mammals;
　　slow-developing creatures, born vulnerable and weak;
　　large-brained, mind-filled creatures: flesh and spirit
　　　　hunting, hurting, hating; longing, laughing, loving:
　　　　knowing (though not knowing) that you love them.
This little fragile thing—
Final creature of them all, cell and primate recapitulating;
burning, blissful Love, condensed to human measure:
babe in manger laid: length, breadth, height, and depth
of stars and cells and souls encompassing:
　　　　such beauty for earth's heavenly food! ·
　　　　such lavish prodigality for humankind, and in it all,
　　　　　because you love it all!

Because of our reward and everlasting gratitude he wants us to have, he is eager to see us pray always. God accepts his servant's intention and effort, whatever our feelings. It pleases him that we should work away at our praying and at our Christian living by the help of his grace, and that we consciously direct all our powers to him, until such time as, in all fullness of joy, we have him whom we seek, Jesus.

(Ch. 41)

'FAITH SEEKING UNDERSTANDING'
Anselm of Canterbury and Julian of Norwich

SISTER BENEDICTA SLG

At first sight Anselm of Canterbury and Julian of Norwich seem to have little in common. The one, a monk from Normandy who became Archbishop of Canterbury under William Rufus, was one of the greatest of medieval scholars, writing his prayers and meditations in beautiful, highly-wrought Latin in the eleventh century. The other, an unlettered laywoman and a recluse in the town of Norwich, wrote (or perhaps dictated) her revelations and meditations on them in English in the fourteenth century. Both composed a short devotional work, however: Julian the *Revelations of Divine Love* and Anselm *The Prayers and Meditations*. It seems clear from these that they both belong to the same tradition of Christian prayer.

In comparing them it is not suggested that there is any actual dependence, for two reasons: first that Julian would not have been able to read the Latin prayers if they had been available to her; and secondly that as a clearly defined body of work they were not available to anyone before the present century. This is because within a few years of Anselm's death the original prayers were surrounded by a host of prayers in the same vein by other writers, all of which were attributed to him. It is only in the past fifty years that the genuine prayers and meditations have again been distinguished in the form in which Anselm meant them to be used, and it is only now that Anselm's teaching as an ascetical theologian can really be appreciated. The body of Anselm's prayers was not available to Julian, but there can be no doubt that she was influenced by the ethos that he had been so largely responsible for creating, and that there are very significant similarities between them. It is of more interest for us to see the same methods, the same approaches, the same understanding in two such dissimilar people, than to attempt any more academic discussion of them. It may be, who knows, that the tradition they both used can be of real significance for us in our same desire for God.

In the first place Anselm and Julian are both people who can truly be called theologians, in the sense of the theologian as one whose prayer is true. Anselm was pre-eminently a theologian, formed by the undivided tradition of Christian doctrine, and bending all the powers of his mind to understanding that faith. This total acceptance of Christian dogma was equally present in Julian, as she says, 'I shall always believe what is held, preached and taught by Holy Church ... it was with this well in mind that I looked at the revelation so diligently' (Ch. 9). In his greatest philosophical work, which is also the greatest of his Meditations, Anselm approaches his search for God in the same way: 'I desire to understand a little of your love, which my heart already believes and loves ... unless I believe I shall not understand' (*Proslogion* Ch. 1). [15] The original title Anselm gave to the *Proslogion* was in fact 'Faith Seeking Understanding', a phrase which sums up his whole approach to theology and prayer, and is as true of Julian as of him.

In both of them there is this complete unity of belief and understanding, the mind at the service of the heart, which makes them truly Christian scholars. To accept the truths of the faith was for them a liberation not a restriction. No one could accuse either of them of being simply echoes of other men's ideas: in both there is originality and personal insight to an astonishing degree. It is to be expected, perhaps, that Julian, whose book-learning was limited, should not have quoted other writers very often; but that Anselm, one of the most learned men of his, or

---

[15] Quotations from St Anselm are taken from *The Prayers and Meditations of St Anselm,* translated by Sister Benedicta Ward SLG (Penguin Classics, 1973).

any age, quoted equally infrequently is more surprising. The Bible, of course, permeated their thought and writings, but even there they rarely quote. They have, it seems, so absorbed and made their own the revelation of God in Christ that they were free to speak for that revelation in terms of their own personality and understanding.

The idea of 'faith *seeking* understanding' is another concept that they have in common—the mobile, flexible, developing nature of faith lies behind their works. Julian reflected for thirty years on the meaning of her revelations, making an interior journey ever deeper into 'the Lord's meaning'. Anselm taught that knowledge of God is a reaching forward and a continuing inner journey: 'Come now, little man, stir up your torpid mind ... flee a while from your occupations ... enter into the inner chamber of your mind ... close the door and seek Him' *(Proslogion* Ch. 1). This inner world of movement and discovery demands for its proper realisation, however, a measure of withdrawal, of solitude, of stillness. It is essentially an interior adventure, made by Anselm in the 'inner chamber', and by Julian in her anchoress's cell.

Firmly based in theological truth, both Anselm and Julian prepared to 'seek understanding' in solitude, and they sought it by paths that are very similar. In both of them there are stages of spiritual progress, stages which were to be most clearly described by St Bernard. At the beginning of the *Revelations* Julian says: 'Through the grace of God and the teaching of Holy Church, I developed a strong desire to receive three wounds, namely, the wound of contrition, the wound of genuine compassion, and the wound of sincere longing for God' (Ch. 2). This threefold pattern of prayer is the same in the teaching of Anselm. It has, of course, a long history in the spirituality of both East and West, but at the end of the eleventh century Anselm articulated it for the West in a new way. Against the background of a liturgically-centred tradition of prayer he set out a way of personal,

interior prayer focussed in the pattern of three wounds, or piercings, of the soul by God. The first wound was that of contrition,
true sorrow for sin and self-abasement; the second wound was
that of compassion, known through the sufferings of Christ; and
the third wound was that of longing desire for God. These three
wounds were to pierce and break the hard heart so that God's
work of prayer could really begin. In each of the Prayers this pattern is followed. It is not a once-for-all way, in which one stage
is finally left behind and then another undertaken; rather it is a
continual pattern of prayer, into which one enters more deeply
all the time.

The first wound that Anselm sets at the beginning of all his
Prayers is that of sorrow for sin and he uses every verbal means
to bring this home to himself: 'I am afraid of my life; for when I
examine myself closely, it seems to me that my whole life is either
sinful or sterile' (Med. 1). 'Alas for my wretched state, how my
sins cry out against me … immoderate offence, offence against
my God' (Prayer to St John the Evangelist, 1). 'The Judge Himself
is my stern accuser and I am clearly a sinner against Him' (Prayer
to St Paul). In Julian there is the same awareness of sin: 'Sin is the
sharpest scourge'; 'holy Church shall be shaken at the world's
sorrow, anguish and tribulation' (Ch. 28); 'the shame that our
foul deeds caused' (Ch. 77).

This awareness of sin and self-abasement is not, in either Anselm or Julian, a matter of psychological or personal guilt; it is
rather a deep theological awareness of the infinite glory of God,
and of the contrast of the horror of any sin which offends against
it. 'How can you call any sin small,' Anselm asks, 'when it is com-
mitted against God?' In Julian it is not reflection upon her own
misdeeds but the sense of 'our foul, black, shameful deeds which
hid the fair, splendid and blessed Lord God' that provokes contrition (Ch. 10).

It is in the second wound, however, that the similarity between Anselm and Julian is most marked: this is their 'compassion' with the sufferings of Christ. The whole of Julian's writing is based on her immediate and vivid experience of the passion of Christ: 'I had,' she says, 'some experience of the passion of Christ, but by his grace I wanted still more. I wanted actually to be there with Mary Magdalene and the others who loved him ... I would be one of them and suffer with him' (Ch. 2). This is Anselm's approach in his Prayer to Christ, an imaginative consideration of the details of the sufferings of Christ which found its ultimate term many years later in the emotions of the Stabat Mater. In the Prayer to Christ he asks: 'Why, O my soul, were you not there to be pierced by the sword of bitter sorrow. ... Why did you not see the nails violate the hands and feet of your Creator? Would that I with happy Joseph might have taken down my Lord from the cross, wrapped him in spiced grave-clothes, and laid him in the tomb.' This desire to experience personally the human side of the sufferings of Christ and of his mother received new impetus from Anselm and coloured the prayers and the art of the later Middle Ages as, incidentally, did his understanding of the tenderness of the child of Bethlehem and his mother. The 'homely', as Julian would say, was seen as an integral part of the 'holy'.

The third 'piercing' for both Anselm and Julian is that of longing desire for the joys of the vision of God. In both writers this theme counterbalances their emphasis on sin, pain and estrangement. In Anselm each prayer ends with a passage full of longing for God and the bliss of heaven: 'He fell asleep in the Lord', he says of St Stephen, 'happy man, to rest in joy and joy in rest; safe home, you are filled with glory, your joy does not change, your light does not fail. ... O rich and blessed peace, how far I am from you; alas for my unhappiness, where I am not, where I am, and, alas, I know not where I shall be.' This theme of the longing of the exiled soul for God lies at the heart of Anselm's understanding of prayer, our restoration to the image of God. This is a fundamental monastic theme in any age which goes with a great longing and a great and positive joy. In Julian there is always this longing for God, and there is also a great deal about joy. It is the joy of God which she sees most of all, his joy in his work of redemption and our joyful response to that work in delight and thankfulness: 'When we are done with grief, our eyes will suddenly be enlightened (Ch. 83); 'we shall partake of God's blessedness forever, praising him and thanking him' (Ch. 85).

One further similarity of these writers in this connection is that 'this holy marvelling delight in God which is love' is expressed in terms of the physical senses. For instance, Julian writes: 'We shall see him truly and feel him fully, hear him spiritually, smell him delightfully and taste him sweetly' (Ch. 43). Anselm frequently uses this sensual imagery, especially about eating or tasting the sweetness of the word of God, and in the last chapter of the *Proslogion* he describes the joys of the saints in terms of the perfect fulfilment of all the senses.

For both Anselm and Julian, the centre and pivot of their approach to God by the three 'piercings' resolves itself into one word—Jesus. In Anselm's first Meditation, when he has thought with anguish of the terror of the Last Judgement, he exclaims: 'But it is he, it is Jesus; the same is my judge between whose hands I tremble. ... Jesus, Jesus, be to me for thy name's sake, Jesus.' Julian says simply: 'I wanted no other heaven but Jesus, who shall be my bliss when I come there' (Ch. 19). The essence of this approach is perhaps found in the Cistercian hymn *Jesu dulcis memoria*—Jesus, the very thought is sweet—but in none of these writers is this concentration on Jesus sentimental or naive. Julian chooses Jesus for her heaven 'whom I saw only in pain at that time'; 'the strength of your salvation, the cause of your freedom, the price of your redemption ... through this, and not otherwise than through this, will you remain in Christ and Christ in you, and your joy will be full' (Meditation 3).

This combination of pain and joy, sorrow and bliss, points to the last and perhaps deepest point of similarity between Anselm and Julian. Their ability to see in the details of suffering the truth of glory is brought out in an unusual and striking way in the concept they share of Christ as our mother. This idea of the maternity of God is found in the Old Testament, and in St Paul, and had found echoes in several medieval writers of the eleventh century; but Anselm gave it a profound and disturbing meaning in his great Prayer to St Paul. He sees St Paul as his mother in the faith, and then turns to apply the same terms to Christ: 'And you, Jesus, are you not also a mother? It is by your death that we have been born; longing to bear sons into life, you tasted death and by dying you begot them.' Christ is seen here as bearing sons by his passion on the cross, a deeper understanding of the meaning of suffering than a simple analogy about the love of Christ being like that of a mother for her children. Anselm sees love as essentially life-giving, not as sentimental or easy. Later in the same prayer he pictures the sinner hiding under the wings of Jesus: 'You, my soul, dead in yourself, run under the wings of Jesus your mother, and lament your griefs under his feathers. Ask that your wounds may be healed and that, strengthened, you may live again.' This is not the gentleness of a mother with a child, but a fundamental concern with our relationship to Christ and the integral meaning of atonement.

Julian expands this theme in several chapters. 'In our mother Christ we grow and develop; in his mercy he reforms and restores us; through his passion, death, and resurrection he has united us to our being' (Ch. 58). And 'Jesus is the true mother of our nature for he made us. He is our mother too by grace, because he took our created nature upon himself' (Ch. 59). Both are saying that Christ bore us as his children by his death on the cross. The pain he suffered was the pain of labour, so that we are his very flesh and blood, and his joy over us is also the cause of all our joy. Moreover, they are making a startlingly modern statement about the nature of God: 'Fatherhood, motherhood and lordship, all in one God', says Julian. 'God is both father and mother', according to Anselm. Not that our images of God are of fatherhood or motherhood, but that God himself contains and completes the whole person. Salvation is a new birth of the whole of humanity by the whole God—all humanity is made whole by the whole of God.

Anselm and Julian were three centuries apart in time and we are six hundred years further on again. The gap of general concepts and culture which lies between them and us is wider than in any other century. Yet they represent an unchanging dimension in the relationship between God and the human being who seeks God, from which we can perhaps still learn. They both accepted the objectivity of God as something other than themselves. In order to seek God, they withdrew into solitude and really set themselves to an *ascesis,* a hard labour, to prepare for finding him. They experienced the sense of their own sin before the glory of God; they found mercy through the new life brought to them by Christ on the cross; they learned to rejoice with all their being in Christ and to long for the bliss of his abiding presence in heaven. For them both the final word is the same: love. Julian, in the last chapter of her book, says that after more than fifteen years of meditation on the revelations it was shown to her that 'love was his meaning'. Anselm, writing in exile forty years after the composition of the Prayers, in his last Meditation came to the same conclusion: 'Thus have you loved me! Draw me to you, Lord, in the fullness of love. I am wholly yours by creation; make me all yours, too, in love.'

FULLNESS OF JOY

Prayer from the *Proslogion* of St Anselm
'When we are done with grief our eyes will suddenly be enlightened.'
Revelations of Divine Love, Ch. 83

My Lord and my God,
my joy and the hope of my heart
tell my soul if this is that joy
which you spoke to us about through your Son,
'Ask and you will receive that your joy may be full'.
For I have found a fullness of joy
that is more than full.
It is a joy that fills the whole heart, mind, and soul,
indeed it fills the whole of a man,
and yet joy beyond measure still remains.
The whole of that joy cannot enter into those who rejoice,
but those who rejoice can enter wholly into that joy.
Speak, Lord, to your servant, in the depths of his heart,
tell him if this is that joy that your servants enter into
when they enter into 'the joy of their Lord'?
But, of course,
that joy in which your chosen ones will rejoice,
'neither has eye seen, nor ear heard,
nor has it entered into the heart of man'.
So as yet, Lord, I have not spoken about or understood
how greatly your blessed ones rejoice.
They will rejoice as much as they love,
and they will love as much as they know.
How much will they know you, Lord,
how much will they love you?
Truly in this life,
'neither has eye seen, nor ear heard,
nor has it entered into the heart of man',
how much they will know and love you in that life.

JULIAN OF NORWICH FOR TODAY

A. M. ALLCHIN

We are living at a time when we need to get a new view of human life in its social, cultural and political aspects, a new view of our own nation and its calling. It is a time which has a desperate need for the renewal of that inner vision, that warmth and understanding which is the outstanding characteristic of the Lady Julian. Technical knowledge and skill, external activities and powers, are multiplied beyond anything that would have been conceivable to our ancestors. But true wisdom, sympathetic understanding of the things of human life, let alone the things of divine life, seems frighteningly lacking. We have a contracted, limited understanding of the nature of the person; little vision of the depths of sorrow and of joy that are open to us, little knowledge of the true coinherence of one with another, little knowledge of what it could be to love God with all our heart, with all our mind, with all our strength, and our neighbour as ourselves. All this we can learn from the Lady Julian.

How is it that she can do this for us? In the main, it is by her quality of life and being, which we share in the pages of her book. She was a woman of great courage and great generosity. It requires both to give oneself to God as completely as she did. And she was a woman of great strength and tenderness. Above all she was a person of a wonderful sanity. People who see visions were not all that rare in the fourteenth century, and we can find them in our own century too. But very often their visions are nothing more than psychological fantasies, projections of their own unconscious fears and desires, which have little or no meaning for others, and which often result in making the visionary self-centred, egocentric, and sometimes even mad.

There is nothing of this in Mother Julian. God showed her things of great terror, as well as things of great joy. She experienced pains and joys of an intensity which we can hardly imagine, but throughout it all she maintains a wonderful humility, a wonderful serenity and objectivity. She can discern between imaginative vision and intellectual, between what she was given and her own reflections upon what she was given. She knows that her revelations were not for herself alone, but for all who are one with her in Christ—for you and for me, no less than for her. Here at the start she teaches us a great lesson about the unity of mankind and about the true nature of prayer:

> The fact that I have had this revelation does not mean that I am good. I am good only in so far as I love God the better; if you love God more than I do then you are by that much better than I. I am not trying to tell the wise something they know already; but I am seeking to tell the uninstructed for their great peace and comfort. And of comfort we all have need. It was certainly not shown me because God loved me more than other lowly souls in grace, for I am quite sure there must be many who have never had any sort of revelation or vision beyond the ordinary teaching of Holy Church, and who yet love God better than I. When I look at myself in particular I am obviously of no account; but by and large I am hopeful, for I am united in love with all my fellow Christians.
>
> It is upon this unity that all those of mankind who are to be saved must depend. God, as I see it, is everything that is good; he has made the whole of creation, and loves all that he has made. And whoever loves his fellow Christians for God, loves all there is. For everything is included in the 'mankind who are to be saved'; everything, I say, that has been created, and the Maker of all as well. For God is in man, and God is in everything. And by the grace of God I hope that anyone who looks at it in this way will be taught aright, and greatly comforted if need be.
>
> (Ch. 9)

In another place she says at one of her 'shewings':

Throughout all this I was greatly moved with love for my fellow
Christians, that they might know and see what I was seeing, for
I wanted it to cheer them too.   (Ch. 8)

What was the heart of this vision of good comfort, this good
news which Mother Julian has to bring to us and to all people?
There are many themes to be followed out as one becomes famil-
iar with her book. But surely one is predominant, both for her
and for us. How is it if God is all-good, all-loving, that the world
is the way it is? How can the pain and sorrow, the sin and the
frustration of our lives be reconciled with what we believe about
the love of God? Lady Julian looked out into her world, and saw
in it cruelty and lust, disease and anxiety, fearful oppression and
fearful waste, and she felt these things with a frightening intensity. And we look out into our world and see similar things. We
might think of the concentration camps of our time, or the return
to the use of torture by nations in Western Europe which seemed
long ago to have given it up. We can see these things as symbols
of the value which we place upon each other, symbols of the fact
that we treat others as if they were of no value at all. Many of our
contemporaries have a sense that there is no meaning in life because of the fear and darkness which has come upon our age. We
also know in our own life and in our own experience of others
how much human beings can wound one another, by their
thoughtlessness, their pride, their blindness, and the way in
which they so often fail to notice the other person. We can make
our own the Lady Julian's words: 'We see deeds done that are so
evil, and injuries inflicted that are so great, that it seems to us
quite impossible that any good can come of them' (Ch. 32).

For Mother Julian this question was not a problem to be dis-
cussed. It was for her a matter of life and death. She lived and
died in this question of the love of God and the sin of man, and
she found the answer not in word and tongue, but in deed and
in truth, in the life-giving death, the suffering and triumph of

Christ into which she entered. So she is able to handle the question with a depth and an insight which it would be hard to rival amongst the greatest theologians of the Church. To the generous love of this East Anglian laywoman, relatively uneducated as she tells us she was, God laid open secrets which have been hidden from the wise and prudent.

> In my foolish way I had often wondered why the foreseeing wisdom of God could not have prevented the beginning of sin, for then, thought I, all would have been well. This line of thought ought to have been left well alone; as it was I grieved and sorrowed over it, with neither cause nor justification. But Jesus, who in this vision informed me of all I needed, answered, 'Sin was necessary, but all shall be well and all shall be well, and all manner of thing shall be well'. In this simple word *sin* our Lord reminded me in a general sort of way of all that is not good; the despicable shame and utter self-denial he endured for us, both in his life and in his dying. And of all the suffering and pain of his creation, both spiritual and physical. For all of us have experienced something of this abnegation and we have to deny ourselves as we follow our Master, Jesus, until we are wholly cleansed. … All this I saw, together with all the suffering that ever has been or can be. And of all pain I understood that the passion of Christ was the greatest and most surpassing. All this was shown in a flash, and quickly passed over into consolation — for our good Lord would not have the soul frightened by this ugly sight.
>
> But I did not see *sin*. I believe it has no substance or real existence. It can only be known by the pain it causes. This pain is something, as I see it, which lasts but a while. It purges us and makes us know ourselves, so that we ask for mercy. The passion of our Lord is our comfort against all this — for such is his blessed will. Because of his tender love for all those who are to be saved, our good Lord comforts us at once and sweetly, as if to say, 'It is true that sin is the cause of all this pain; but all shall be well and all shall be well, and all manner of thing shall be well'. These

words were said most tenderly with never a hint of blame either
to me or to any of those to be saved. (Ch. 27)

On one occasion the good Lord said, 'All shall be well'. On another, 'You will see for yourself that all manner of thing shall be
well.' In these two sayings the soul discerns various meanings.
One is that he wants us to know that not only does he care for
great and noble things, but equally for little and small, lowly and
simple things as well. This is his meaning, '*All* shall be well'. We
are to know that the least thing will not be forgotten. Another is
this: we see deeds done that are so evil, and injuries inflicted that
are so great, that it seems to be quite impossible that any good
can come of them. As we consider these sorrowfully and mourn-
fully, we cannot relax in the blessed contemplation of God as we
ought. This is caused by the fact that our reason is now so blind,
base and ignorant, that we are unable to know that supreme and
marvellous wisdom, might and goodness which belong to the
blessed Trinity. (Ch. 32)

Perhaps it will be thought that this is too easy, this apparent
optimism that 'all shall be well'. As we read the Lady Julian we
see that it was not at all easy for her. This assurance was won
through much suffering, through her share in the Passion of
Christ himself. Again it may be asked, is there not something
here which is contrary to the clear teaching of the Church and the
evidence of the Gospels with their stern words about the reality
of judgement, and the final separation of good from evil? Is not
the seer at this moment setting herself up against the teaching of
the Church? At no point, it must be said, does she show greater
wisdom and discretion than this, a wisdom and discretion which
one could have wished the theologians had always followed. On
the one hand she puts what her Lord had showed her about the
restoration of all things, and on the other the common teaching
of the Church, and refuses to suppress either—thereby expressing by an unresolved antinomy the full mystery of the end of

humanity as it is revealed to us in the fullness of our faith. I quote
again:

> The consideration of this I found most marvellous, and in my
> wonder I thought about our faith; our faith is grounded in God's
> word, and part of it is that we who believe in that word of God
> will be saved—completely. Another part of our same belief is
> that many creatures will be damned; for example, the angels
> who fell from heaven through pride, and are now fiends; and
> those men on earth who die apart from Holy Church, namely,
> the heathen; and those too, who are christened but live unchris-
> tian lives, and so die out of love—all these shall be condemned
> to hell everlastingly, as Holy Church teaches me to believe.
>   This being so, I thought it quite impossible that everything
> should turn out well, as our Lord was now showing me. But I
> had no answer to this revelation save this: 'What is impossible to
> you is not impossible to me. I shall honour my word in every
> respect, and I will make everything turn out well.' Thus was I
> taught by God's grace to hold steadfastly to the faith I had al-
> ready learned, and at the same time to believe quite seriously
> that everything would turn out well, as our Lord was showing.
> For the great deed that our Lord is going to do is that by which
> he shall keep his word in every particular, and make all that is
> wrong turn out well. How this will be no one less than Christ can
> know—not until the deed is done.   (Ch. 32)

It is interesting to read, after these words of a great contemplative of the Middle Ages, a comment on them from a great
contemplative of our own day. In *Conjectures of a Guilty Bystander*
Thomas Merton writes:

> I pray much to have a wise heart, and perhaps the rediscovery
> of Lady Julian of Norwich will help me ... She is a true theologian
> with greater clarity, depth and order than St Teresa: she really
> elaborates, theologically, the content of her revelations. She first
> experienced, then thought, and the thoughtful deepening of ex-
> perience worked it back into her life, deeper and deeper, until
> her whole life as a recluse at Norwich was simply a matter of

getting completely saturated in the light she had received all at once, in the 'shewings', when she thought she was about to die.

One of her most telling and central convictions is her orientation to what one might call *an eschatological secret*, the hidden dynamism which is at work already and by which 'all manner of thing shall be well'. This 'secret', this act which the Lord keeps hidden, is really the full fruit of the Parousia. It is not just that 'He comes', but He comes with this secret to reveal, He comes with this final answer to all the world's anguish, this answer which is already decided, but which we cannot discover (and which, since we think we have reasoned it all out anyway) we have stopped trying to discover. Actually, her life was lived in the belief in this 'secret', the 'great deed' that the Lord will do on the Last Day, not a deed of destruction and revenge, but of mercy and of life, all partial expectations will be exploded and *everything* will be made right. It is the great deed of 'the end' which is still secret, but already fully at work in the world, in spite of all its sorrow, the great deed 'ordained by our Lord from without beginning'.

She must indeed believe and accept the fact that there is a hell, yet also at the same time, impossibly one would think, she believes even more firmly that 'the word of Christ shall be saved in all things' and 'all manner of thing shall be well'. This is for her the heart of theology: not solving contradiction, but remaining in the midst of it, in peace, knowing that it is fully solved, but that the solution is secret, and will never be guessed until it is revealed.

To have a 'wise heart', it seems to me, is to live centred on this dynamism and this secret hope—this hoped-for secret. It is the key to our life, but as long as we are alive we must see that we do not have this key: it is not at our disposal. Christ has it, in us, for us. We have the key in so far as we believe in Him, and are one with Him. So this is it: the 'wise heart' remains in hope and in contradiction, in sorrow and in joy, fixed on the secret and the 'great deed' which alone gives Christian life its true scope and dimensions! The wise heart lives in Christ.   (pp. 191–2)

The life and activity of such a one as Julian of Norwich does not finish with her death, for the lives of such people create the holy places, which remain places of God's presence and God's love. Their words come down to us charged with the life and power and the healing of eternity. They pass a judgement on much of what in our age we take for granted. Our lives do not consist in our outer activities, our outward possessions, but in what we are in ourselves. Lady Julian renounced all opportunities for what we call 'useful work', and so carried on a work of greater value to human life than any other. She did not have the fulfilment of married life, but yet she is mother to an innumerable family. She shut up all her life into the narrowness of one room, but because that room was open to God, the maker and redeemer of humanity, she was able to embrace every person and the whole world in her thought, in her care and in her love. She had been freed from that prison of self-preoccupation which can follow us wherever we go, however far we go. By her life she tells us that God is, and God is to be worshipped, and that God is our only complete and final end. And she tells us that God can be known and loved here in this place and now in this time. By the richness of her writing, with its mingling of earth and heaven, of what is holy and what is homely, of grace and nature, she shows us that it is only in and through the light of God that we can ever fully appreciate or enjoy the world which God has made and our own small life within it. For all this we stand with praise and thanksgiving before God, to whom, like all the saints, she constantly points us

It is sooth that sin is cause of all this pain;
but all shall be well, and all shall be well,
and all manner of thing shall be well.